Loud Larry

Written by Larry Dane Brimner • Illustrated by JoAnn Adinolfi

Published in the United States of America by The Child's World®
PO Box 326 • Chanhassen, MN 55317-0326
800-599-READ • www.childsworld.com

Reading Adviser

Cecilia Minden-Cupp, PhD, Director of Language and Literacy, Harvard University Graduate School
of Education, Cambridge, Massachusetts

Acknowledgments

The Child's World®: Mary Berendes, Publishing Director

Editorial Directions, Inc.: E. Russell Primm, Editorial Director and Project Manager; Katie Marsico,
Associate Editor; Judith Shiffer, Assistant Editor; Matt Messbarger, Editorial Assistant

The Design Lab: Kathleen Petelinsek, Design and art production

Library of Congress Cataloging-in-Publication Data

Brimner, Larry Dane.
  Loud Larry / by Larry Dane Brimner ; illustrated by JoAnn Adinolfi.
     p. cm. — (Magic door to learning)
  Summary: Larry learns the difference between loud and quiet while getting to know his newborn
sister.
  ISBN 1-59296-530-X (lib. bdg. : alk. paper) [1. Noise—Fiction. 2. Babies—Fiction. 3. Brothers and
sisters—Fiction.] I. Adinolfi, JoAnn, ill. II. Title.
  PZ7.B767Lou 2005
  [E]—dc22   2005005368

A book is a door, a magic door.
It can take you places
you have never been before.
Ready? Set?
Turn the page.
Open the door.
Now it is time to explore.

Larry was **LOUD.**

4

When he walked, it was **LOUD**.
When he sang, it was **LOUD**.
He even whispered **LOUD**.

Then one day his mother
and father brought home a
baby sister.

"Say hello to Louise,"
said his father.

Louise was little.

She was wrapped in a
red blanket so that only
her face peeked out. She
was sound asleep.

"HELLO, LOUISE," said Larry, and when he did Louise jumped wide awake and cried.

She cried the biggest
cry Larry had ever
heard. It was so big, it
was **LOUD.**

She made such a
ruckus that Larry had
to cover his ears. Even
then Louise was still
LOUD.

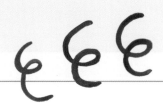

"WHAT A RACKET!"
said Larry.

"Try holding her," said Larry's mother.
"Try walking with her," his father suggested.

13

Larry tried holding her.
Larry tried walking with
her. But when Larry
walked it was **LOUD.**
Louise cried even
LOUDER!

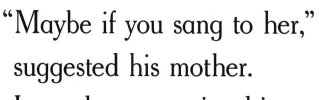

"Maybe if you sang to her,"
suggested his mother.
Larry began to sing his
favorite song.

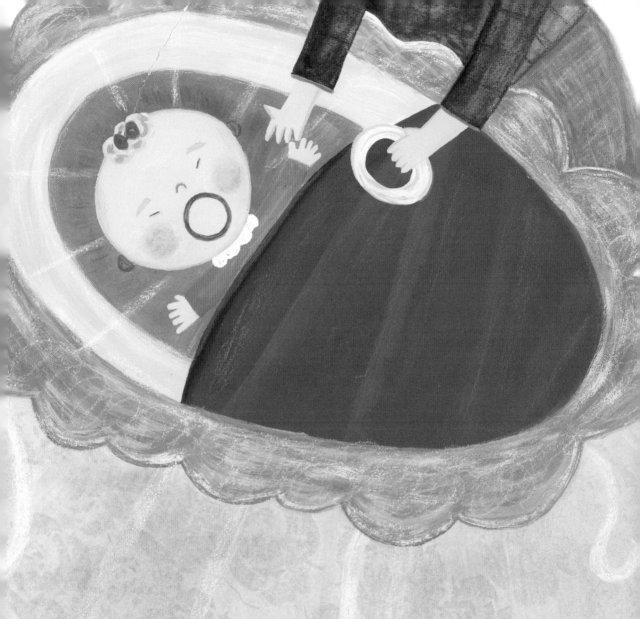

But when he sang, it was **LOUD.**

So Louise cried even
LOUDER.

"Maybe if you
whispered," said Larry's
father.

Larry started to
whisper, but then he
had an idea.

"Louise is a little baby," he said.

"I will whisper a little baby whisper."

It was the littlest baby whisper he could make.

It was such a little baby whisper that it was quiet.

It was so very, very
quiet that Louise was
soon fast, fast asleep.

Our story is over, but there is still much to explore beyond the magic door!

Are you a good whisperer? Play a game of Telephone! Sit with your friends in a circle. Begin by whispering something to the person next to you. Players should pass along the message this way until it ends up back with you again. Is it the same message you began the game with?

These books will help you explore at the library and at home:

Carle, Eric. *The Very Quiet Cricket*. New York: Philomel Books, 1990.
Laguna, Sophie, and Kerry Argent (illustrator). *Too Loud Lily*. New York: Scholastic Press, 2004.

About the Author

Larry Dane Brimner is an award-winning author of more than 120 books for children. When he isn't at his computer writing, he can be found biking in Colorado or hiking in Arizona. You can visit him online at *www.brimner.com*.

About the Illustrator

JoAnn Adinolfi lives in New Hampshire and has two children who can be a lot like Loud Larry. While JoAnn paints her pictures, she sometimes likes to sing real loud. But shh . . . don't tell anyone!